On or Under
Where's Eddie?

Daniel Nunn

Illustrations by Steve Walker

Raintree

Chicago, Illinois

Hide and Seek

www.capstonepub.com
Visit our website to find out more information about Heinemann-Raintree books.

To order:
☎ Phone 800-747-4992
💻 Visit www.capstonepub.com to browse our catalog and order online.

Edited by Dan Nunn, Rebecca Rissman, and Sian Smith
Designed by Joanna Hinton-Malivoire
Picture research by Mica Brancic
Originated by Capstone Global Library. Ltd.
Production by Victoria Fitzgerald
Printed and bound in United States
012320   003162
16 15 14 13 12
10 9 8 7 6 5 4 3 2 1

Library of Congress Cataloging-in-Publication Data
Nunn, Daniel.
  On or under : where's Eddie? / Daniel Nunn.
    p. cm.—(Hide and seek)
  ISBN 978-1-4109-4711-6 (hb)—ISBN 978-1-4109-4717-8 (pb) 1.
English language—Prepositions—Juvenile literature. I. Title.
  PE1335.N86 2013
    428.2—dc23   2012003789

Acknowledgments
We would like to thank the following for permission to reproduce photographs: Shutterstock pp.5 (© Ingrid Prats), 6 (© NeonLight), 7 (© Andrii Ospishchev), 8 (© Adisa), 9 (© Alexander Chaikin), 10 (© Ihnatovich Maryia), 11, 12 (© Worachat Sodsri), 13, 14 (© Ronald Sumners), 15, 16 (© Kirill Vorobyev), 17, 18 (© Chin Kit Sen), 19, 20 (© iadams), 21 (© Breadmaker), 22 (© Alexia Khruscheva), 23 (© Dmitry Rukhlenko).

Front cover photograph of a tractor reproduced with permission of Shutterstock (© NanoStock).

Every effort has been made to contact copyright holders of any material reproduced in this book. Any omissions will be rectified in subsequent printings if notice is given to the publisher.

Contents

Be careful when you hide!
Eddie can hide in places where people can't. Hiding inside things can be very dangerous. Always ask an adult if it is safe first.

Meet Eddie the Elephant

This is Eddie the Elephant.

On

Sometimes Eddie hides **on** things.

Under means below something.

Find Eddie!

Can you find Eddie?
Count to 10, then off you go!

Eddie is **on** the table.

Where is Eddie? Is he on the bridge or under the bridge?

13

Eddie is **under** the bridge.

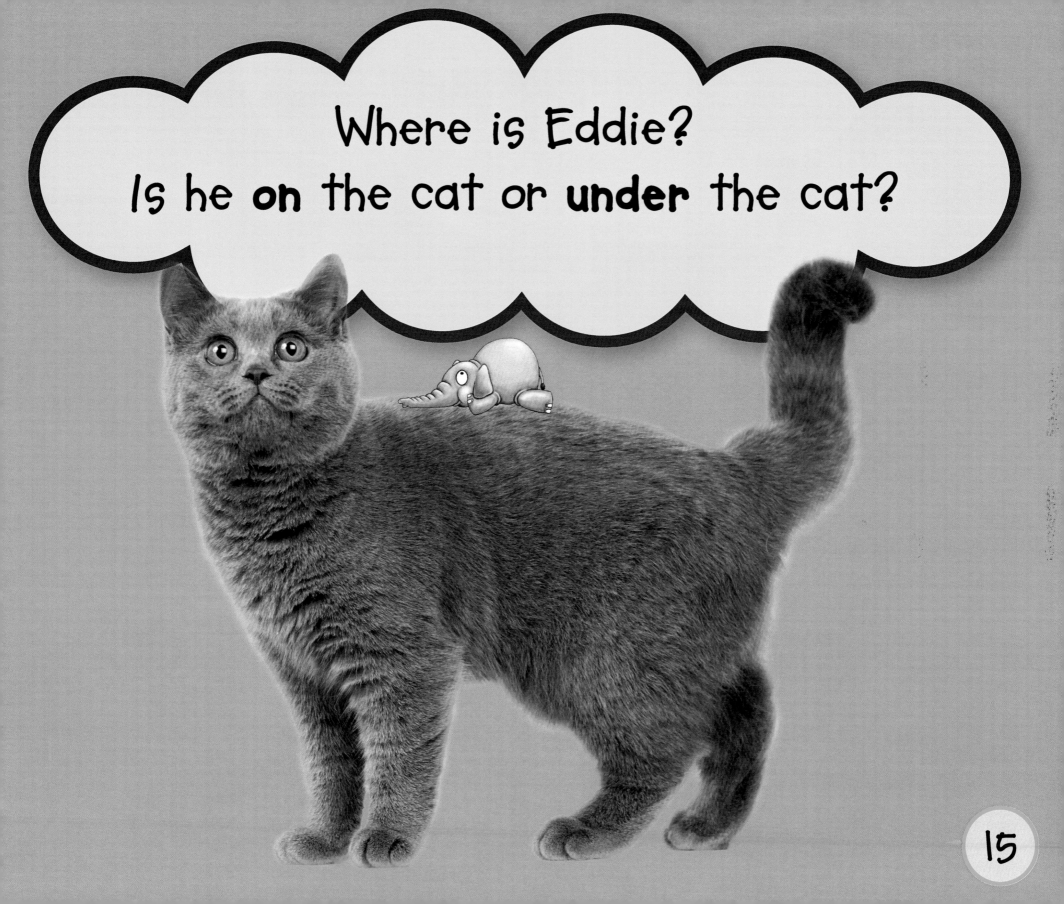

15

Where is Eddie? Is he **on** the yellow pillow or **under** the yellow pillow?

Eddie is **under** the yellow pillow.

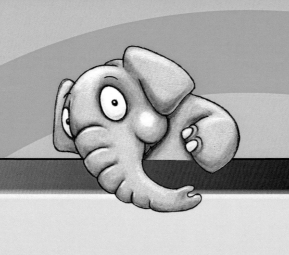

Where is Eddie?

Is he **on** the television or **under** the television?

Eddie is **on** the television.

True or False?

1. Eddie is **under** the bed. True or false?

You can find the answers on page 24.

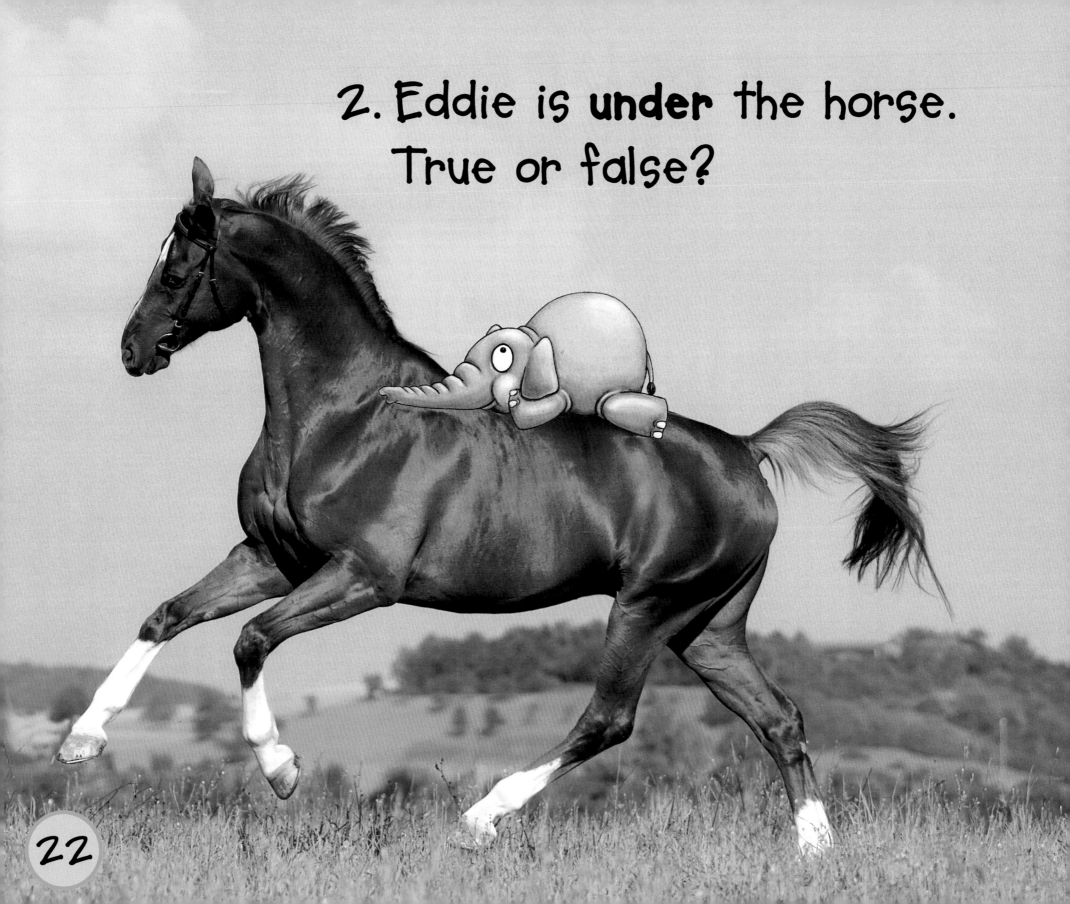

2. Eddie is **under** the horse.
True or false?

3. Eddie is **under** the hat. True or false?

Answers and More!

True or false?

1. True! Eddie is **under** the bed.
2. False! Eddie is **on** the horse.
3. True! Eddie is **under** the hat.

Where can Eddie hide next?

Look around the room you are in.

What could Eddie hide **on**?

What could Eddie hide **under**?